The Early Intervention Handbook

Intervention in Literacy

Greg McMillan, The City of Edinburgh Council,
Education Department

Moira Leslie, Moray House Institute of Education

·EDINBVRGH·
THE CITY OF EDINBURGH COUNCIL

EDUCATION

First published in 1998 by
The City of Edinburgh Council
Education Department
George IV Bridge
Edinburgh EH1 1UQ

ISBN 1 902299 00 0

Contents

Introduction 5
Why Early Intervention? 5
What Factors Promote Reading Success? 6
Reading, Enjoyment and Comprehension 8
From Theory into Practice 10
Recommendations for Pre-school 10
Recommendations for the Early Years of School 10
Time on Task 11
Concepts of Print 12
Developing Phonological Skills 13
Rhyming 13
Alliteration 14
Activities to Develop Awareness of Rhyme and Alliteration 14
Rhyme, Alliteration and Learning Letters 16
Teaching Using Sound Picture Cards and Plastic Letters 17
Using Phonological Skills in Early Reading – Learning by Analogy 19
Building Skills through Rime and Analogy 19
Rhyming Words 21
Common Words 23
Common Words List 25
Developing a Sight Vocabulary 26
Writing at the Early Stages 28
Developing Writing through Play 28
Resources for the Home Corner 29
The Three-pronged Approach to the
Development of Writing at the Early Stages 30
Spelling 36
Simultaneous Oral Spelling 36
Parental Involvement 37
Paired Reading 38
Paired Reading – A Guide for Parents 40
How to Do it 40
Reading Recovery 42
Assessment 43
New School Entrants 43
Assessment in the Early Years of Schooling 44
Planning Issues in Early Intervention 46
Staff Development 46
Curriculum 46
Resources 46
Parental Involvement 46
Community Links and Involvement of Other Agencies 46
Deployment of Staff 47
Reading Recovery 47
Assessment 47
In-school Coordinator 47
Regular Review Meetings 47
Books and Materials 48

Acknowledgements

This handbook draws on the theoretical work of a number of writers, particularly Marilyn Adams, Linnea Ehri, Lynette Bradley, and Usha Goswami.

The authors would like to thank the many colleagues who have helped in developing this handbook, in particular Diana Fox, Diane Pepper and Helen Fraser.

Although too numerous to mention individually, the authors would also like to thank the teachers and children for their hard work and enthusiasm in early intervention projects in Edinburgh and elsewhere in Scotland.

Introduction

This handbook is written for teachers, nursery nurses and all those involved in fostering early reading acquisition. It is based on the research conducted by the authors since 1991, their experience in organising and evaluating early intervention projects and developing education authority policy on reading.

The handbook examines some current research in reading acquisition and relates this to classroom practice. While some of the intervention strategies will be familiar, it is the combination of approaches and the strong links between theory and practice which have proved successful in promoting early literacy attainments.

Why Early Intervention?

'We need to intervene as early as possible. This requires a general re-thinking as regards current policy in many areas, where resources are allocated to children who have already failed.'
Peter Bryant and Lynette Bradley

'My research carries the rather depressing message that as you start, so you finish. The gap between good and poor readers widens as time goes on. Make sure you give children a good start!'
Morag Stuart

'It seemed to me that the longer we left the child failing the harder the problem became.'
Marie Clay

In recent years there has been a consensus among educational researchers that children who make a poor start in reading tend to continue to have difficulties in spite of subsequent programmes of remediation. It has also been shown that it is possible to predict, to some extent, the likely future success of children in learning to read long before they enter school.

While some children have specific learning difficulties which lead to poor progress in reading, it is important to remember that the largest vulnerable group is not such children, or children with sensory deficits, or children who have been poorly taught. In fact, what many poor readers have in common is a relatively impoverished home background. Children who come from a disadvantaged family, live in a disadvantaged neighbourhood, or attend a school with many disadvantaged children tend to have depressed attainments. However, 'social disadvantage' is too broad a concept to explain reading failure and for all children it is important to consider what factors may lead to success or failure in reading.

What Factors Promote Reading Success?

The process of learning to read is developmental and does not start on entry to school. The well prepared child enters school with a wealth of experience and skills in reading-related activities. The earliest prediction of reading success is the child's knowledge of rhyme and phonology (that is, the sounds in spoken language). It has been shown that children who can recite nursery rhymes at age three are statistically more likely to make good progress with reading on school entry. It has been demonstrated that this is because knowledge of nursery rhymes leads on to an understanding of the phonological principles of language – that words consist of sounds and these sounds can be split, manipulated and combined. If the child also has knowledge of letters, these skills can be combined to give an insight into the structure of written words. This insight will help not only with 'phonic' word attack but will also help with recognition of the visual letter patterns of words.

The well prepared child's impressive array of skills will have been gained through years of pre-school exposure (and often individual tuition from a parent) to books and language activities. Many such children can recognise all the letters of the alphabet, can write a few words, such as their name, can read some familiar words, often from environmental print, can split the initial sounds from words (as in I-spy) and have extensive knowledge of rhyme. These important phonological and alphabetical skills are, however, just one aspect of pre-school reading preparation. The child may have had the experience of listening to many stories and sharing many books, playing word games, operating a computer, and so on. He will be familiar with many of the conventions of print, will have developed a love of books and a desire to read. At the earliest stages reading stories aloud to children is the most important activity. It is not, however, just reading to children that leads to subsequent linguistic development and reading progress. Children need opportunities to discuss the meanings of words. Before children enter school there must be a commitment to provide these opportunities. Children need to learn about the phonemic composition of words and be taught the letters of the alphabet and their phonemic significance. Such instruction must take place in a stimulating literacy environment where they are surrounded by attractive books, displays, friezes and charts.

The Primary 1 class teacher will generally find it straightforward to build on the extensive literacy experience that well prepared children bring to school. Reading acquisition will be rapid and, often, apparently effortless. Some children, however, will have had little preparation and support and schools face a huge task in compensating for limited pre-school experience. On entry to school the amount of time children spend on literacy activities is a crucial determinant of progress. The more time they spend working on the skill, the more rapid the progress, However, perversely, children with poor home support and difficulty with reading are likely to read much less than their more successful peers. Not surprisingly, the gap widens unless there is a programme of intervention. Time spent reading at home and at school is a major factor in reading progress.

Reading can also be boosted by early experience of independent writing. Trying to puzzle out or invent the spellings of words while writing makes children attend closely to, and think about, the structures of words. The skills thus developed spill over into reading. While most children learn to read irrespective of the precise teaching method, large-scale studies in the United States have shown that the most successful programmes include systematic phonic and code emphasis skills, closely associated with regular opportunities for meaningful connected reading. Other interventions have demonstrated that children also benefit from specific teaching of very high frequency common words. A small number of words (for example, *the, of, and, a*) make up 50 per cent of all written English. Learning such words builds confidence and gives children a flying start.

Finally, it has been shown that the quickest and most effective help for children experiencing difficulty is to provide early individual tuition. While this may be difficult for the busy classroom teacher, such help can at times be provided by learning support teachers, volunteers and parents at home.

To summarise, early literacy intervention should promote:

- parental involvement and support
- exposure to a culture of literacy
- knowledge of concepts of print
- knowledge of rhyme
- knowledge of phonology
- knowledge of letter names
- time on task/time spent reading text
- early experience of independent writing
- early help for children with difficulty
- individual tuition where possible
- regular, meaningful connected reading with associated phonic instruction
- automatic recognition of the most common words

Many of these activities start at a pre-school level.

Reading, Enjoyment and Comprehension

The most fundamental activity in the teaching of literacy is storybook reading. Children do have to learn about letters and sounds and start to visually recognise letter strings. However, long before they reach this stage they should have been read many stories and poems and should have started to develop a love of books. Learning to read words and sentences is only a step towards being able to read independently for pleasure. Children should be read stories from the earliest age and this should continue at home, in nursery and in school up to and beyond the stage at which they themselves are fluent readers.

Letter and word recognition and phonological activities should take place alongside reading of meaningful connected text and should not become an end in themselves. Children should not have to learn a set of word or letter recognition skills prior to being given access to reading books. Reading is for pleasure and for acquiring information. Learning about how written language works should enhance this process.

However, it is important to distinguish between decoding and comprehension. Comprehension is the purpose and the end of the reading process. Decoding is the simple act of identifying the words in a sentence. If the word in the initial reader is often predictable by referring to the picture, the child may assume that words are understood by looking at pictures. When a reader reads a word by saying a synonym that bears no similarity to the written word (for example, 'fine' for 'good') he demonstrates an overdependence on context and meaning at the expense of accuracy. Reliance on contextual cues is a characteristic of beginning and poor readers and, as a strategy for decoding words, breaks down rapidly as texts become more difficult. The more successful early readers recognise the primacy of print and may in fact make errors by reading 'words' which make no sense but are close to the letter string in the word (for example, 'strig' for 'string'). It is important that children realise that in skilled reading the word is first decoded and then its meaning is discovered. Decoding is vital to initial reading and, in some respects, comprehension is a more general language skill. A sentence which has been read is similar to a sentence which has been spoken. If the child has sufficient language skills to understand the spoken sentence, he can also understand the sentence which has been read.

Comprehension skills are however also important in self-correction and error recognition. Language skills are vital both for the comprehension of speech and written material. However, just as hearing precedes comprehension the central issue in reading is not teaching the child to understand, but teaching the child to decipher words that are to be understood.

Decoding is not the **purpose** of reading. The aim is to extract a message or story from the print. Beginning readers can and should use meaning and context to check the accuracy of their attempts at word recognition or decoding. What they should not do is rely on context and meaning and neglect to attend to the detail of print. It is crucial for good reading comprehension that the child has quick and accurate word recognition skills. The more mental effort that a child has to put into identifying or sounding out letter sequences, the less mental capacity is left to attend to meaning. Children with automatic word recognition skills also have better reading comprehension.

In reading acquisition there is reciprocal causation. Phonological skills are vital in word recognition but learning to read itself improves phonological skills. In the same way, language skills are necessary for reading comprehension and reading contributes to linguistic development and comprehension skills. In some ways it is artificial to separate out the skills of reading. Humans often process information in parallel not sequentially. The child must bring all his skills – linguistic, phonological, visual, experiential – to the reading task in a spirit of active enquiry.

From Theory into Practice

The body of recent research on the acquisition of literacy skills and the importance of early intervention strategies has wide ranging implications for practice in both nursery and the early stages of school. If this research is to inform and develop the teaching of literacy skills, then it is necessary to analyse and translate these findings into specific activities and approaches which can be implemented in the classroom.

The following recommendations, used in recent early intervention initiatives, are a result of such an analysis and can be used as a framework to develop the teaching of literacy. It is important to stress that these recommendations will be implemented in the context of a literacy-rich environment in which children are encouraged to develop their enjoyment of all aspects of reading and writing.

Recommendations for Pre-school

- Children should hear books being read on a daily basis.
- Children should be given a wide range of experiences to develop their concepts about print.
- Children should be given experiences to develop awareness of the sounds in spoken language.
- Every effort should be made to stimulate children's interest in, and knowledge of, letters.
- Children should be encouraged in their attempts at early writing.
- Parental involvement and support should be actively promoted.

Recommendations for the Early Years of School

- Every child's reading should be heard daily.
- Children should be taught about the concepts of print.
- Every child should be taught the letters of the alphabet.
- Children should receive training in sound awareness combined with work on analogies and word patterns.
- Children should be given the opportunity to write independently from the earliest stages.
- Children should be taught to read the most common words.
- A specific method of spelling instruction should be used. Simultaneous oral spelling is recommended.
- Parental involvement and support should be actively promoted.

Time on Task

Every child's reading should be heard daily.

In many ways this is the most crucial factor in literacy acquisition. Think again of the well prepared child with his thousands of hours of literacy preparation before entering school. Compare the prospects of a child who has learned about books, stories, rhymes, letters, writing, and so on, with those of a child who enters school devoid of such experience. On entry to school and in the early years it has been shown that the amount of time spent on reading is closely connected with progress. This may seem very obvious. The more one practises a skill, the more efficient one becomes. A recent study found the main difference between 'gifted' young musicians and their peers was that the gifted children practised more often. However, in reading instruction it is often the children who need the most practice who get the least. Children who find reading easy take to it effortlessly and are soon reading school books, library books, comics, menus, cereal packets and so on. Children who do not find reading easy may be unable to read without help and will often need individual teaching. These same children may receive limited exposure to reading material at home. Classroom observations have repeatedly demonstrated 'the Matthew effect' (the rich get richer as the poor get poorer). More able readers tend to read more and less able readers to read less. Studies in the USA have suggested that good readers spend 20 times as much time reading as poor readers. The gap therefore widens between the good and poor readers.

Early intervention is important in providing a high level of literacy stimulation (time on task) in order to avoid children acquiring a sense of failure. Every effort must be made to ensure that children spend time being involved with books from an early age. At school age, children require to have reading heard very regularly both in the classroom and at home. The time that children actually spend on supervised reading with an adult is vital to their progress. Every means of increasing the amount of time the child spends engaged in this activity should be explored. Increasing parental support, using volunteers, peer tutoring, deploying nursery nurses and allocating learning support time are some of the options available. Time spent on other literacy activities is also vitally important – hearing stories, writing and dictating stories, work on rhyme and many others. It is important to remember that the 5–14 National Guidelines indicate that up to 35 per cent of time can be devoted to language activities, including work across the curriculum. While teacher-supervised reading is the cornerstone of any programme of literacy instruction, many pieces of literacy-related language work can take place as part of cross-curricular activities. For example, there is no shortage of number rhymes which introduce early maths concepts while also teaching rhyme, alliteration and possibly recognition of number names.

Concepts of Print

Children should be taught about the concepts of print.

Children need an essential understanding of the nature, purpose and value of print – sometimes described as 'basic print awareness'. Without this awareness they will make little use of any alphabetic or phonological knowledge which they may have. Children's knowledge of basic print concepts is a strong predictor of the ease with which they will learn to read in the early years of schooling. They have to begin to understand the format of books – that language is represented by print, that print is invariant, that letters build up to form words, that spaces separate words and that print reads left to right. They need to realise that stories come from the print, not the pictures. Many young children are confused by concepts such as *word*, *letter* and *sentence*. They often use *word* and *letter* interchangeably, do not realise that words on the page (unlike spoken language) are discrete units and sometimes think that a line is a sentence (as it often is in initial reading books).

Adults can help children to develop concepts about print by talking about how books are put together, demonstrating writing, using big books where children can see the printed words as they are read, encouraging children to make their own books and to attempt writing.

There are a number of ways of assessing knowledge about concept of print. The best established test is by Marie Clay but there is a range of other commercially produced tests which can be used with small groups.

Developing Phonological Skills

Children should be given experiences to develop awareness of the sounds in spoken language.

Phonological awareness is the child's ability to segment spoken words into their constituent sounds. While this is a purely oral skill, it is an important predictor of how well children will learn to read and spell. Children who have problems with phonological skills almost always have difficulty in learning to read.

It has been shown that many three-year-olds can judge that two words rhyme and that there is an association between this ability and their knowledge of nursery rhymes. It has also been shown that training children in sound categorisation tasks can lead to more rapid progress when reading instruction begins.

There are several levels of phonological awareness. In the past it was thought that spoken words could be broken up into either **syllables** or **phonemes**. Thus a word like *painter* could be divided into two syllables, *paint* and *er*. Phonemic division is harder. A phoneme is the smallest meaningful unit of sound in a word. *Hit* and *fit* both contain three phonemes and differ by one phoneme. Small children can often divide easy words into syllables but have great difficulty with breaking up words into phonemes. Until they start to read, few children can cope with phonemic segmentation. However, there is another level of phonological awareness which falls between the syllable and the phoneme. Words can be divided into the **onset** and the **rime**. The onset consists of the initial consonant or consonants and the rime consists of the vowel and any final consonants. Thus *hit* and *fit* have onsets of *h* and *f* respectively, but share the same rime of *it*. With a word like *chair*, the onset is *ch* and the rime is *air*. The rime of *fight* is *ight*. Children can distinguish rimes and onsets before they begin to read and long before they can cope with phonemic splitting or blending. As will be discussed later, there is a strong relationship between knowledge of rimes and onsets and the acquisition of reading and spelling.

At the nursery stage phonological awareness is best developed through traditional activities, such as nursery rhymes and word games. Young children enjoy learning rhymes and alliterative word games and such activities fit in well with nursery routines. Learning nursery rhymes may help to develop an enjoyment of books and foster auditory memory in addition to developing an awareness of rhyme.

Rhyming

From nursery level children should have access to a range of simple rhyming books, including big books, nursery rhyme audio-tapes and rhyme posters. They should be taught to memorise and act out well-known rhymes. Parents can be involved by asking them to teach rhymes and jingles at home or to tell the children about traditional skipping rhymes. Children can learn modern rhymes in, for example, advertising jingles and contrast them with traditional rhymes.

Alliteration

The ability to detect and produce alliteration can be fostered in a similar way using games, tongue twisters, jokes and labels.

The following range of activities and games can be used to develop rhyme and alliteration.

Activities to Develop Awareness of Rhyme and Alliteration

These ideas can be used with children from the nursery to Primary 3 stage. Obviously the more complex games and activities involving written material are more suitable for older children.

Rhyme
- Teach traditional nursery rhymes.
- Ask the children to act out the rhymes, illustrate them and use puppets to enact them.
- Ask children to recite rhymes in groups and as individuals.
- Make audio-tapes of the children reciting rhymes.
- Provide tapes for children to follow nursery rhymes in books and big books.
- Recite rhymes but miss out the rhyming word and ask the children to supply it.
- Play spot the deliberate mistake by putting in non-rhyming words, for example 'Humpty Dumpty sat on the fence'.
- Make classroom displays of nursery rhymes. These can be related to project and topic work. Write the words in large letters.
- Make class books of favourite rhymes.
- Teach playground and skipping rhymes and games.
- Teach traditional question and answer rhyming games.
- Play dancing and chasing games with changes of direction when rhyming words are chanted.
- Teach number rhymes.
- Make up your own variations, for example, 'Two, four, six eight, these are the things I really hate...'.
- Make number rhyme books, friezes and displays.
- Recite, invent and act out count down rhymes, for example, 'Ten green bottles standing on the wall, one fell down and knocked out Paul'.

- Invent new words for songs and rhymes.
- Compare traditional rhymes with children's favourite modern songs.
- Make up raps.
- Invent limericks.
- Teach simple rhyming slang.
- Invent families of invented animals and monsters with rhyming names.
- Play a rhyming version of 'I-spy'.
- Play with rhyming riddles, for example, a pet that rhymes with 'fat'.
- Play rhyming snap and rhyming lotto with pictures.
- Play odd one out games with pictures or objects – one of which does not rhyme.
- Play Kim's Game with rhyming objects or toys or pictures.
- Ask the children for words that rhyme with their names, or their friends' names.
- Make feely bags and ask children to find rhyming pairs of objects.
- Have a rhyming display with objects and pictures which all rhyme.

Alliteration

- Have a display of alliterative objects and pictures.
- Teach and make up tongue twisters, for example, 'The ragged rascal ran round the rugged rock'.
- Make up a class alliterative book based on children's names, for example, 'Wayne wears wellies'.
- Have a letter/sound of the week and ask children to bring in objects and pictures starting with the chosen letter.
- Ask children to describe themselves alliteratively – 'big Barry', 'silly Simon', etc.
- Share alliterative counting with children and make up your own – 'two terrible tigers'.
- Invent alliterative descriptions – 'big bears', 'wet windows', 'happy hairdressers'.
- Make alliterative alphabet books using names, 'Awful Alex', 'Boring Brian', or animals, 'Active Ants', 'Brave Bears'.
- Make up alliterative advertising slogans like, 'Buster's Bread is best'.
- Play listing games, for example, Grandmother Went to Market, with alliterative words.
- Play snap and lotto with alliterative pictures.
- Play odd one out with picture cards – two with alliterative names and one without.
- Make feely bags with objects starting with particular sounds. Ask the children to identify the objects by touch.
- Sort objects into categories according to the initial sounds.
- Look for as many things as possible in a picture or book which start with the same sound.
- Play ' I-spy'.
- Play Kim's Game with alliterative objects.

Rhyme, Alliteration and Learning Letters

Every child should be taught the letters of the alphabet.

Many of the activities which develop alliteration and rhyme can include the use of written words and letters. It has been shown that linking phonological work to written letters at a very early stage leads to much better progress than phonological work in isolation. Large-scale assessments have indicated the vital importance of letter recognition in early reading. Children who cannot recognise all, or almost all, letters automatically and with ease invariably have difficulty with reading and spelling. However, it is not enough simply to teach children to name letters, either by sound or alphabetic name. They must also understand the function of letters – that words are made up from letters, that letters and letter combinations represent all the sounds of spoken language, and that spoken words can be broken up into constituent sounds (see Concepts of Print, page 12, and Developing Phonological Skills, page 13).

The following activities can be used to encourage children to relate rhyme and alliteration to printed letters.

- Play snap, lotto and so on using written words.
- Use a big book of rhymes to help children discover that rhyming words have the same group of letters at the end.
- Children can make an alphabet scrapbook and choose pictures to illustrate each letter.
- Children listen to stories from books and pick out the words that start with a particular sound.
- Have a letter of the week table where children put objects or pictures which start with a particular letter.
- Write rimes and onsets on different cards. Ask children to see how many words they can make using different onsets with the same rime.
- Make onset and rime word wheels.
- Encourage children to trace words and to write letters and words in wet sand.
- Play magnetic fishing using rime and onset cards.
- Sing the Alphabet Song and alphabet jingles.
- Display alphabet friezes, commercially produced or made by children or parents.
- Encourage children to play with alphabet tiles and mats. These can be used for simple matching, spelling out words and names and even hop-scotch type spelling games.

- Stack trays in alphabetic order.
- Play alphabet bingo.
- Make sure that nursery and early years classrooms have plenty of alphabet books, jigsaws and games.
- Use computer keyboards and alphabet and rhyme-related software.
- Make posters with a collection of pictures representing a particular letter, for example boy, bus, bat, ball, bag for b.
- Make personal alphabet dictionaries.
- Make a wall hanging with alphabetically labelled pockets. The children can collect pictures of things beginning with each letter and put them in the pockets. At later stages this can be used as a key words dictionary.

Teaching Using Sound Picture Cards and Plastic Letters

The teacher will require a set of pictures which both demonstrate simple **rhymes**, for example *hat, cat, rat, bat*; *sun, gun*; *bed, red*; *can, man*; and **alliteration**, for example *pin, pen, peg*; *can, cat, cot*. It is important, and not always easy, to find words which can be clearly represented pictorially and will be in the spoken vocabulary of almost all children of a given age. Children can then work on categorising these cards according to rhyme and initial sounds and playing games such as finding the odd one out. At the earliest stage, sound categorisation games can be played without any linkage to alphabetic letters. For many school-age children linking sound discrimination with letters will lead to more rapid progress. However, it makes no sense to attempt to teach 'phonics' to children who are unable to discriminate between sounds orally.

Plastic letters can be useful in learning letter sounds. They are bright and attractive and can be handled, encouraging a multi-sensory approach. Children who have trouble writing clearly can form words. Plastic letters are always the same size and do not vary like written print.

Sound Picture Cards

Take a set of pictures which all start with the same sound. Ask the child to select two cards and say the words. Repeat the words emphasising the initial sound clearly. Point out that both words begin with the same sound. Mix the two sets of cards and go through the following steps:

1   Find me a picture that begins with *f* (the spoken sound).
2   Find me a picture that begins with *s*.
3   Find all the pictures that begin with *s*. Find all the pictures that begin with *f*.
4   Put out three *f* pictures and one *s* picture. Ask the child to find the odd one out.

When letters are being introduced, children can be asked, at this stage, to choose a card. The teacher can then spell the word using plastic letters. The child chooses another card with the same first sound and the teacher again spells it out. The child chooses a third card and is asked to find the correct initial plastic letter. The teacher then makes this word. The child is helped to see that all three words start with the same letter. This process can be repeated with all the alphabet letters and consonant digraphs.

Plastic Letters and Rhyme

As soon as a child can make a few simple words, he should, if he has some knowledge of rhyme, be able to generate many more written words.

The child chooses a picture card and, with help if necessary, makes the word with plastic letters. The child then picks another rhyming card and makes the new word. While often the child will start afresh, he can be shown that only the first letter need be changed. Words can then be formed without reference to the sound picture cards, in the following way:

1   The child makes a familiar word, for example *hat*, with plastic letters.
2   The child, with help if necessary, thinks of a rhyming word, for example *cat*.
3   The child changes the first word into the second word. The process is repeated with other rhyming words. The fundamental point that the child must recognise is that the *at* part of the word remains the same.
4   The words made should be copied into a word book for use in the child's own writing.

Plastic letters can also be used to help in building new, phonetically regular words:

1   The child names the word he wants to spell, for example *went*.
2   He selects the first letter, *w*.
3   He then repeats the word and tries, with help, to stop at the next sound, *we*.
4   This is repeated until the child has spelt the whole word correctly.

The advantage of using plastic letters is that any errors can be altered quickly, leaving no trace.

Once the child has learned a new word by this process, the word can be reinforced by activities such as tracing, using a paint brush and water to make a disappearing word on the blackboard, writing the word in word books, tracing the word in sand. Only a few words need to be learned in this way. Once the child can spell *went*, he should then use his knowledge of rhyme, backed up by a list of rhyming words if necessary, to form words like *tent, bent,* and *sent*. This teaches the more useful skills of reading by **analogy**.

Using Phonological Skills in Early Reading – Learning by Analogy

Children should receive training in sound awareness combined with work on analogies and word patterns.

Many studies have demonstrated that explicitly relating phonological tasks, games and activities to alphabetic letters leads to accelerated progress. It appears that a knowledge and understanding of rhyme and alliteration enables children to make connections between spelling patterns when they start to learn to read. The child who can detect **onset** and **rime** can use this skill to make analogies between words. This can apply to difficult, non-regular words such as *light*. If this is seen as onset (*l*) and rime (*ight*) the child has a means of attacking 90 English words (*fight, right, might, bright, flight*, etc) and, in both reading and spelling, a consistent pattern emerges. At a simpler level, a child who can read the word *hat* and who has basic skills of rhyme and alliteration, should be able to read a large number of words (*fat, rat, bat, cat*, etc) by analogy. Children can use both rimes and onsets to make such analogies. Thus they may make an onset analogy between *str-ap* and *str-ip* and *str-eet*. It appears that there is a logical developmental progression in young children, starting with early experiences and knowledge of rhyme, moving on to awareness of rime and onset units, and culminating in the use of analogies in reading and spelling.

Ultimately, children will develop instant visual recognition of familiar letter strings (for example, *ight*). This demonstrates the way in which orthographic (visual) and phonic skills are complementary and develop in parallel. This is a contrast to the traditional view which regarded 'look and say' and 'phonics' as alternatives.

Reading by analogy may be particularly useful for children with difficulties, as analogies use the rime-onset level of phonological knowledge which is easier for young children than the traditional phoneme blending and splitting approach.

Building Skills through Rime and Analogy

One way to help children recognise analogies between words is again to use plastic letters. These can help both at the phonological and the orthographic level. Using tangible, brightly coloured letters may help children remember sound-symbol relationships and make discrimination between similar letters easier. Also it is easy for teachers to demonstrate an invariant rime or onset. For example, a rime such as *eat* can be formed out of plastic letters and left intact, while words such as *heat, seat, neat, beat, peat* are formed. Children who have good oral, phonological skills can move easily to this kind of activity. For other children this work can be combined with the use of picture cards (see Developing Phonological Skills, page 13). After categorising several pictures by rhyme, the child would be shown how to form the word with plastic letters, for example, *cat*. The child would then select a rhyming card, for example, *hat*, and be asked to make this with plastic letters. The teacher can demonstrate how only one letter needs to be changed.

Teaching by analogy using plastic letters should often start using a word the child already knows. Words which consist of a rime with no onset, such as *and* may be particularly easy to use. Thus the child may be asked to form this word using the plastic letters. Next the child should be asked to say another word with a similar sound, for example, *hand*. The child then tries to change *and* into *hand*. Some children may find this difficult. If they are only given a small choice of onset consonants such as *s, b, h* from which to choose, this may simplify the task. The important point is that the rime *and* remains constant and this should be repeatedly pointed out to the child. As the child is dealing initially with single consonant onsets and rime 'chunks', the difficult single phonemic blending task is avoided. With progress, children may use two or three consonant onsets (or consonant blends) such as *sh, st* and *str*.

Plastic letters may also be used for more conventional blending tasks. A child may be asked to spell out *fat* using the letters and saying *f, fa, fat*. The common rime *at* can then be developed.

The list of rhyming words on pages 21–22 is useful for teachers and pupils in developing phonological work.

Rhyming Words

at	bun	cow	ice	ace
bat	run	how	mice	face
cat	sun	now	rice	race
chat	fun		twice	space
fat		be	nice	
mat	day	he	lice	feet
sat	hay	me		meet
rat	pray	she	and	sheet
that	say	we	band	
	stay		hand	no
an	way	top	grand	go
can	spray	chop	land	so
fan	tray	hop	sand	
man		pop	stand	all
nan	hen	mop		ball
pan	men	shop	ate	call
ran	pen	stop	date	fall
van	ten		gate	hall
than	then	brown	hate	tall
	when	clown	late	small
big		down		
pig	bet	town	bad	ought
rig	get		dad	brought
wig	jet	back	glad	bought
	let	black	mad	thought
car	met	pack	sad	
far	net	sack		bed
jar	pet		each	fed
tar	set	brown	beach	red
star	wet	clown	reach	led
		down	teach	shed
class	cot	town	breach	
glass	dot			book
grass	got	sock	right	hook
	hot	block	bright	cook
by	lot	clock	fight	look
cry	not	rock	light	took
dry	rot	lock	might	shook
fly	spot	knock	night	
my			sight	eat
	bee	long	slight	beat
bell	see	song		heat
well	three	strong	for	meat
shell	tree	wrong	or	seat

bell	moon	blew	bake	bent
fell	soon	flew	cake	lent
sell	spoon	knew	make	dent
tell	noon	new	rake	sent
well		threw	snake	tent
smell	ill		take	went
	bill	did	lake	
ear	chill	hid		bring
dear	fill	lid	blame	king
fear	pill	rid	came	ring
hear	spill		game	sing
near	will	bump	name	string
year	hill	jump	same	swing
		lump	fame	wing
end	out	hump		
bend	about		again	air
lend	shout	in	pain	chair
friend	spout	bin	rain	fair
mend		chin	train	hair
send	say	win	strain	pair
	day	thin	drain	stair
bug	hay	sin		
mug	spray	tin	broke	cried
hug	pray		choke	died
rug	tray	alone	spoke	fried
		bone	woke	tied
ill	brick	phone		tried
hill	lick	stone	fine	
pill	pick		line	ink
fill	sick	chalk	mine	pink
bill	stick	walk	pine	sink
till	quick	talk	wine	think
spill	tick	stalk	twine	drink
thrill				stink
	bride	coat	cast	
good	ride	goat	fast	brave
hood	side	boat	last	cave
stood	hide	moat	mast	gave
wood	tide		past	save
food	slide	blow		wave
old		grow	keep	slave
cold	been	know	sheep	
gold	green	show	deep	
sold	queen	snow	sleep	
told	seen	throw	steep	

Common Words

Children should be taught to read the common words.

The common words are those high frequency words which make up the greatest percentage of all written text in the English language and the reader will regularly encounter them in books, magazines or newspapers. They include short function words like:

that	the	in
there	they	is
this	then	it

The 100 common words make up 50 per cent of all printed material that a reader will encounter in books, magazines or newspapers.

Beginning readers who are still in the pre- and partial alphabetic phases of development (see Developing a Sight Vocabulary, page 26) can have great difficulty with these words which are often visually similar, and are difficult to associate with an idea or image.

However, it is essential that children do learn to read these words as soon as possible, or they will experience great difficulty in making sense of any written material. The aim, therefore, is that children will be able to read these words instantly, automatically and effortlessly. It is also necessary for the young writer to be able to spell these words quickly and accurately and so it is recommended that they feature regularly in spelling practice.

Systematically teaching the common words in the early years of schooling, through active involvement in a range of activities and games, will help to develop children's confidence as independent readers and writers.

Teachers using any of the commercially produced reading schemes as a resource will recognise most of the common words as being similar to the Key Words in the reading scheme. The gradual introduction and repeated use of these high frequency words in the children's reading books is a very effective strategy for helping beginner readers to learn them.

When teaching the common words, it will be necessary to link this to the children's alphabetic knowledge, phonological awareness and growing understanding of reading and writing by analogy.

Many of the common words can be used for rime and onset work, for example the words *and*, *in* or *it* are the rimes of many other words which the child will come across in text, or wish to write.

In the following lists of words the onset changes but the rime (which is one of the common words) remains constant.

	and		**in**		**it**
h	and	p	in	p	it
l	and	t	in	f	it
b	and	sp	in	m	it
s	and	ch	in	s	it
str	and	th	in	k	it

Common Words List

First 20	Second 20	Third 20	Fourth 20	Fifth 20
a	at	up	my	play
to	or	them	some	over
and	one	will	must	went
of	be	who	her	an
the	this	which	like	want
is	from	me	into	here
you	have	she	has	so
in	by	an	look	these
he	had	do	go	many
it	him	big	no	then
that	were	how	could	than
was	but	their	did	been
are	not	if	who	day
with	all	word	will	put
as	when	out	now	over
on	your	made	little	by
for	we	them	other	our
his	with	more	did	out
they	can	then	come	down
I	if	there	make	be

25

Developing a Sight Vocabulary

Over the years there has been much confusion over sight reading and how best to develop this fundamental skill. At various points it has been implied that sight words are somehow 'photographed' and recalled through a purely visual method or that the shape of the word is crucial in recall. These notions did not take account of the fact that skilled readers can recognise a word irrespective of changes in typeface or whether it is in lower or upper case. Clearly what the reader is, in fact, doing is recalling a sequence of letters.

Linnea Ehri, who has done much of the valuable work in this area suggests that a connection-forming process is at the heart of sight word learning. Connections are made between the written forms of words and their pronunciations and meanings. This information is then stored in the reader's word memory bank. It is not the case that effective sight word learning involves memorising the shape or other visual features of words and has nothing to do with letter-sound correspondence. Equally, it is mistaken to think that only irregular words are read by sight or that sight reading has something to do with the flash card method of teaching children. Normally readers acquire sight words through encountering them in texts which are being read. It is usually necessary to see the same word 4–6 times before it is established in the reader's lexicon.

Different types of connection will predominate at different points in the child's development as a reader. Ehri describes four stages – pre-alphabetic, partial alphabetic, full alphabetic and consolidated alphabetic.

In the pre-alphabetic phase the beginning reader remembers how to read sight words by forming connections between some visual attributes of words and their pronunciation or meanings and then storing these in memory. This can be done by remembering 'book' as the word with two eyes in the middle or even by a mark on the page next to a printed word. Eventually environmental print may be recalled by the shape of a logo. This may lead to print being connected to an idea and young children may read, for example, 'Crest' as 'toothpaste'.

Early readers, who have some knowledge of letters and phonology, start to remember how to read sight words by forming partial alphabetic connections between some of the letters in written words and sounds detected in their pronunciations. Typically, beginning readers will first use initial letters, then initial and final letters and later still some of the middle letters. While this phase will still lead to many errors with confusion between similar words (fat/fit, ground/grand) it is much more effective than the visual cue reading of the pre-alphabetic stage.

At the full alphabetic phase beginners remember how to read sight words by forming complete connections between the letters of a word and the phonemes detected in its pronunciation. For example, the word SPOON has five letters but only four phonemes – S, P, /U/ and N. The child is likely to decode the word but, after a few trials, will bond the letter sequence S, P, OO, N to the phonemic structure of the word and will be able to recall the word instantly from his bank of sight words.

In the final phase, which Ehri calls the consolidated alphabetic phase, the reader retains complete information about the spelling of sight words in memory. By consolidating letters into larger units (-tion, intro-, para- con-, etc) they can use familiar letter patterns to enable rapid growth of their sight lexicons as they encounter many different words in their reading.

It is therefore important to realise that the old dichotomy between phonics and sight reading is quite artificial. Children need to attend to letter/sound sequences in both phonic attack and sight reading. Indeed, phonically decoding a word is a useful way of developing a sight memory for it. It is also important to remember that children need to see the same word several times before it is likely to become a sight word. The same words, therefore, must appear fairly regularly in their reading material.

Writing at the Early Stages

Children should be given the opportunity to write independently from the earliest stages.

From the earliest stages, it is essential that children are given a range of opportunities to become involved in writing, as well as reading activities. It is important that children are also encouraged to discuss the links between reading and writing and that situations arise where children see a range of purposes for writing.

Many children will experiment with writing long before they begin to read and these early attempts at writing are now recognised as a vital stage in their literacy development.

Developing Writing through Play

Play situations at nursery and the early stages of school will provide a range of meaningful contexts for writing, where an audience and a purpose will motivate the children to produce their own early attempts at writing.

Setting up real-life and imaginary contexts in the classroom, where the use of print-related resources and a range of writing materials are an integral part of the play, encourages children to demonstrate and develop their understanding of the purpose of reading and writing. Teacher involvement in modelling the writing and reading process will be an important strategy in supporting the children's literacy development.

Play contexts to promote writing could include:

- a home corner
- a cafe
- a hairdresser
- a hospital
- a garden centre
- a garage
- a pet shop
- a tourist office
- a bookshop
- a library
- a post office
- a toy shop

The literacy play in these meaningful contexts encourages the children to imitate different forms of writing which they have observed at home and in school, for example writing letters, signs, shopping lists, bills and greeting cards. In this way they have the opportunity to demonstrate and develop their understanding of the range of uses of literacy in real-life situations.

When writing is the planned focus for curricular development, the resourcing of these areas should reflect this and the children should have access to a wide range of literacy materials which they can use in their play.

Resources for the Home Corner

An example of this approach would be the following selection of print and writing materials which are to be found in a real home:

- storybooks
- information books
- poetry books
- newspaper delivered daily
- magazines
- comics
- address book
- diary
- telephone book
- recipe book
- catalogues
- shopping lists
- greeting cards
- blank paper
- note pads
- envelopes
- computer
- letters and advertising leaflets delivered daily
- pens
- pencils
- markers
- crayons
- chalk and board
- highlighters
- magnetic letters
- coloured post-its
- wrapping paper for addressing parcels
- sellotape

The Three-pronged Approach to the Development of Writing at the Early Stages

As well as planning for play contexts to develop literacy skills, a structured approach to the teaching of writing at the early stages is essential. One method which involves a number of strategies has proved to be highly successful in recent early intervention initiatives. This method, now known as the Three-pronged Approach, focuses on the three elements of independent writing, scribing and copying.

Independent Writing

This describes children's own attempts at writing which will range from scribbles, letter-like forms, actual letters (often from their own name), invented spellings, conventional words, or a combination of these.

Encouraging and praising these early attempts at writing is of paramount importance if children are to develop as independent writers who have the confidence to 'have a go' at unknown words. It is also necessary to work closely with parents, so that they too realise the importance of these first steps which their children are taking on the continuum of writing development.

Time should be spent encouraging individual children to read back what they have written and inviting them to articulate and discuss why they wrote certain words as they did.

Scribing

This describes the process of the teacher acting as a scribe for a group of children or an individual child. The child discusses what he wants to write with the teacher, and the teacher writes the words for the child. This process of modelling writing has many benefits for the young writer who has the opportunity to observe a piece of writing building up, with the words being formed letter by letter in front of them.

This will also be the first stages of drafting for the child, as the teacher will not necessarily write down the first thing that the child says, but will discuss, at an appropriate level, issues such as who the audience is, the purpose of the writing and the content. Through involvement in this active process the children will be encouraged to realise they can come back to a piece of a writing and that it can be worked on and improved.

Copying

This describes the approach in which the child creates a short piece of writing using either a class or personal bank of word cards. The child, working alone or with teacher support, selects the relevant words from the word bank, places them in the correct order and then copies them onto a page. Before using a bank of individual words with the child, the teacher can introduce this approach by scribing what the child wants to write on a long strip of paper, asking the child to read what he has written, and cutting the sentence into two or three parts. She then asks the child to put the sentence back together and re-read it before copying it out on paper. During this process the child is actively involved in reading, selecting, ordering and writing words.

It is important to stress that the practice of the teacher merely writing a sentence which the child then copies on the line below is not recommended, as it is quite possible for the child to complete this task with a minimum of involvement in the process and no real interaction with the words on the page.

Independent Writing, Scribing and Copying – the Combined Approach

The three elements in this approach should be used together to promote the development of writing at the early stages. For example, a child may begin a story by writing independently, at whatever stage he has reached on the writing continuum, and the teacher might then scribe the rest, or the child could begin by copying a story created by using individual word cards and end it by adding a piece of independent writing. In some cases all three elements of the approach will be used in one piece of work.

It is the combination of these elements which seems to be successful, as each activity supports the other, with children learning about the writing process from different perspectives.

The examples of children's work on pages 32–35 demonstrate the combined approach to the teaching and learning of writing at the early stages.

Example 1

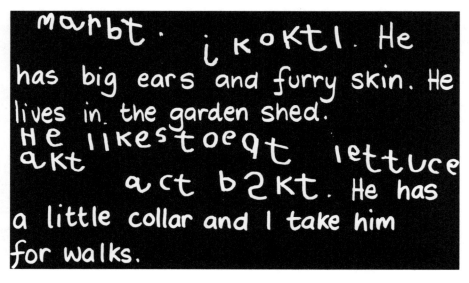

marbt.   i koktl. He
has big ears and furry skin. He
lives in. the garden shed.
He likestoeqt   lettuce
akt   act b2kt. He has
a little collar and I take him
for walks.

marbt.   i koktl.   He

Independent writing
My rabbit is called Kittle.

has big ears and furry skin. He
lives in. the garden shed.

Scribing
He has big ears and furry skin. He lives in the garden shed.

He likestoeqt   lettuce

Cōpying
He likes to eat lettuce

akt   act b2kt.

Independent writing
and carrots and cat biscuits.

He has a little collar and I take him
for walks.

Scribing
He has a little collar and I take him for walks.

Example 2

ILYCDWehaɥɾɟɾeɒjdocz
because you learn words and you
hear good stories.
I like Wot Now Bernard
the bestofall Itisa
really goodstory.

ILYCDWehaɥɾɟɾeɒjdocz

Independent writing
I like it when we are reading books

because you learn words and you

hear good stories.

Scribing
because you learn words and you hear good stories.

I like Wot Now Bernard
the bestofall Itisa
really goodstory.

Copying
I like 'Not Now Bernard' the best of all it is a really good story.

Example 3

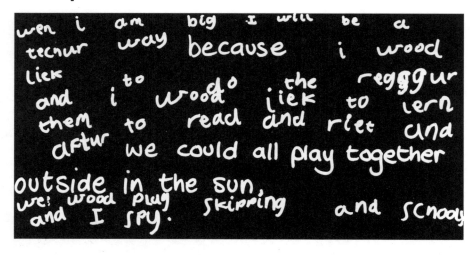

wen i am big I will be a
tecnur way

Independent writing
When I am big I will be a teacher. Why

because

Scribing
because

Independent writing
I would like to do the register and I would like to learn them to read and write and after

we could all play together outside in the sun
Scribing
we could all play together outside in the sun.

we! wood play
Independent writing
We would play

skipping and scnooly and I spy.
Copying
skipping and schools and I spy.

Example 4

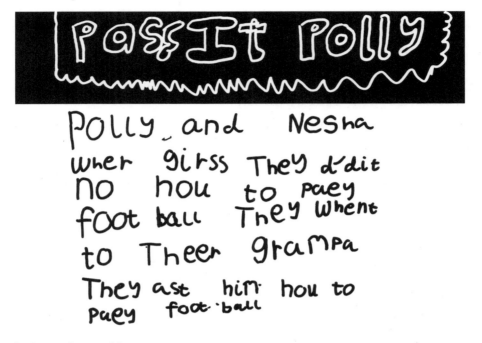

Independent writing

Polly and Nesha were girls. They didn't know how to play football. They went to their grampa. They asked him how to play football.

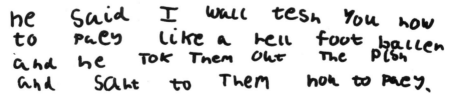

Copying

Granpa said that long ago he used to be a football player. He used to play for the Scottish army team.

he Said I will tesh You how
to puey like a rell foot ballen
and he Tok Them Out The Plsh
and Saht to Them hou to puey.

Independent writing

He said I will teach you how to play like a real footballer and he took them out to the pitch and showed to them how to play.

Spelling

A specific method of spelling instruction should be used.

Simultaneous Oral Spelling

Research suggests that this is the most effective method of structured spelling instruction. The method has the following steps:

- Write or form the word with plastic letters.
- Write the word saying each letter in turn. The child, therefore, sees each letter, hears it spoken, and also receives kinaesthetic feedback through the movements of writing and speaking. The multi-sensory approach maximises recall.
- Check that the word is correct.
- Cover the word and repeat the process twice more.

Ideally, the word should be practised three times per day for several days, though realistically this may be difficult to achieve. Obviously, this intensive method of learning will be used for making a start with children who are having difficulty or to introduce new and unfamiliar spellings. Once children can spell a particular word, they should always be encouraged to use generalisation and analogy to discover how to spell other words in the same word family.

This variant of look–cover–write–check was devised by Gillingham and Stillman.

Parental Involvement

Parental involvement and support should be actively promoted.

The level of parental involvement in children's learning is closely related to academic success. All parents are keen to see their children do well. However, they may need guidance on what activities are likely to be helpful. Teachers need to develop the confidence of parents as educators of their children. There is a mythology prevalent among many parents that they should not help their children to learn to read, in case they get it wrong and cause confusion. It is clear that the reverse is the case. Children whose parents show them the words as they read books together, whose parents teach them to recognise letters and to count, do better at school irrespective of whether the parents' teaching style coincides with that of the school. Children who are exposed to knowledge from different sources take advantage of this.

Parents are in an ideal position to teach their children as individuals. They know them well and are motivated to help. Their praise and interest are highly rewarding for the child. Ideally, they provide a literacy-rich environment and models of adults who have a love of books. Not all parents can or will be able to make use of all these factors. However, schools must look on parents as a resource and make plans to involve them as much as possible from an early stage.

Suggestions for Involving Parents
- Recruit parents to read stories in the nursery.
- Ask parents to teach their children a nursery rhyme. Involve them in the nursery activities to promote letter recognition and phonological awareness.
- Start an after-school story reading club for parents and children.
- Take parents and children on library visits.
- Produce advice packs on helpful activities for parents at nursery and Primary 1 entry.
- Train parent volunteers for shared reading.
- Have a specific homework policy which is shared with parents. Send reading books home regularly.
- Invite parents to Paired Reading meetings and enlist them to embark on this programme. (A Paired Reading guide is provided on pages 40–41.)
- Encourage parental involvement in school in general. Parents who come to social events are more likely to attend other meetings.
- Have a particular member of staff with a remit for fostering parental involvement.

- Where possible, a policy of home visiting may involve many parents who would be unlikely to attend meetings in school.
- Establish links with agencies such as Adult Basic Education who may have family literacy initiatives in your area or useful information.

A small number of schools have home-link and home-visiting staff who work with them. This is invaluable in developing links between parents and schools and other agencies.

However, parental involvement *per se* is not enough. Parents must be actively involved in encouraging and fostering specific literacy skills. For school-age children and their families the Paired Reading approach has proved to be effective.

Paired Reading

It has been shown that the most effective strategies in teaching reading include close monitoring, individual attention and immediate feedback and error correction. Paired Reading is a simple and effective method of parental involvement which meets these criteria. It is also a useful balance to some of the other ideas and suggestions made earlier as Paired Reading places a clear emphasis on the enjoyment of storybook reading, on reading continuous text and on comprehension skills. As Paired Reading leads to increases in time spent reading and promotes parental involvement, it fits in well with the aims of early intervention.

The specific techniques of Paired Reading – free choice of storybook, individual supervision, an emphasis on error-free continuous reading, reading together and reading alone are outlined in the Guide for Parents, pages 40–41. In Paired Reading children are asked to pursue their own interests in reading and there is an emphasis on understanding. Paired Reading emphasises continuity and eliminates stopping to puzzle out individual words. This frees children to devote their attention to the meaning of the text and speeds up the whole reading process. While phonological and word attack skills are vital, they must be taught in a context of opportunities for rapid, meaningful reading for pleasure. Paired Reading provides this. The child is also working with a perfect example of adult reading. The child hears words pronounced correctly which may help with syllabification skills. When reading with parents, children will gain in motivation through this support and interest.

Studies have shown that setting up a scheme need not be particularly elaborate or time-consuming. A short presentation to parents with two or three video clips, a brief talk and the distribution of a Guide to Parents seems quite adequate. It is important that the school ensures that there is a wide range of attractive books available for the children. The School Library Service may be able to assist with this. Typically a six- to ten-week period of Paired Reading leads to very substantial gain in both reading accuracy and comprehension for participants. Paired Reading also reduces stress for parents and children.

The main problem in organising Paired Reading projects may be attracting parental interest, particularly in areas of disadvantage. However, every effort that can be made by schools is worthwhile.

If recruiting parents is difficult, it is worth considering schemes with a few volunteer adults coming into school and doing Paired Reading with children. Many schools have initiated peer tutoring with older pupils doing Paired Reading with younger children. It has been shown in some cases that this will help the reading of both children.

In summary, Paired Reading is a simple, quick and economical method which accelerates reading progress and leads to spin-off benefits with parental involvement in the child's schooling.

Paired Reading – A Guide for Parents

Paired Reading means reading aloud with your child. It is a good way for parents to help their children and is popular with the children. Studies all over the world have shown that Paired Reading works well and many children have taken part with good results.

How to Do it

Choosing Books

In Paired Reading the children choose the books they want to read. Do not worry if they choose a book that seems too easy or too difficult, they will soon learn to pick suitable books. Any book that catches your child's interest is a good choice. Books may come from home, school or the local library. If your child gets tired of a particular book and wants to change it, you should let him do so. After all, that is what adults do when they read for pleasure. Make sure that your child has a wide choice of exciting books. Remember any book the child chooses is suitable. Comics, newspapers and magazines are fine.

Time

Try to read with your child for 10 to 15 minutes a day at least 5 days a week. Do not do more than this unless your child is very keen. Do not choose a time to read when your child really wants to do something else, for example, in the middle of a favourite TV programme.

Place

You will need a quiet place. Your child will not be able to concentrate if there is a lot of coming and going or if the TV is on. Sit comfortably and close to your child.

Reading Together

You and your child both read the words out loud together at the same speed. When you get to a word your child cannot read or gets wrong, just read the word for him and get him to repeat it. Make sure your child points at each word as he reads. This way he will not lose his place and it helps you to read along at the right speed.

Reading Alone

When your child thinks he can manage to read part of the story on his own he should tap the table or squeeze your arm. At this signal you stop reading and let the child read on by themselves. When your child makes a mistake or gets stuck just tell him the word, get him to repeat it and start reading together again.

Mistakes

Don't pay too much attention to mistakes, everyone makes them! Don't get angry and upset as this will just put your child off reading. Don't try to make your child sound out and spell the word, just tell him what the word is and get him to repeat it. The whole point of Paired Reading is to encourage reading stories with as few interruptions as possible.

Do praise your child often. Praise your child for getting words right and simply correct mistakes.

Talking

Every now and again, at the end of a page or a short section of the book, stop and talk about the story. Ask your child what he thinks is going to happen next. Show an interest in the story.

Main Points

1 Let your child choose the book.
2 Let him point to the words. Read at the child's speed.
3 If your child makes a mistake, say the word for him.
4 Use lots of praise and make reading fun. If you do not seem to enjoy reading, neither will your child.
5 Discuss the story with your child.

Reading Recovery

Dame Marie Clay has devoted many years to the development of an early intervention programme aimed at pupils with reading difficulties. Typically, the Reading Recovery programme involves identifying children with difficulties after one year of schooling. The pupils are assessed through the reading of simple books and tested for alphabetic knowledge and individual word reading. The child's understanding of print and their writing ability are recorded. Reading Recovery is a preventative programme which aims to bring children up to average class levels of attainment in a time-scale of 12–20 weeks. Clay emphasises that the intention is to equip children with skills which will enable them to continue to progress when they return to class. The pupils selected for Reading Recovery work for half an hour per day, on an individual basis with a specially trained teacher. They work from a menu of tasks which usually includes reading two or three familiar books and a new book. The teacher may work on letter identification tasks and word analysis skills arising from the books which have been read. Writing is an integral part of the programme. The Reading Recovery programme is set out in detail in Clay's book *Reading Recovery: A guidebook for teachers in training*. This new revision includes a greater emphasis on phonological skills than previous versions.

While a full Reading Recovery programme can only be conducted on an individual basis by a learning support specialist, there are many ideas, for example for developing letter identification, which are helpful for all children. Clay's emphasis on the importance of re-reading familiar books is relevant to all children in developing fluency and comprehension skills. Clay also makes the important point that, whether children are using a graded reading scheme or other books, they should be able to read 90 per cent of the words for independent reading and 80 per cent of words at the instructional level. If children are given books which are too difficult, they will rapidly reach frustration and lose comprehension of the text.

Assessment

New School Entrants

As the best predictors at the pre-school stage of later success in acquiring literacy are knowledge of phonology and knowledge of letter names, it makes sense to assess these areas. It has also been shown that simple concepts about print predict reading success to some limited extent, at least in the first year or so of formal instruction.

Assessing Knowledge of the Alphabet

This can be simply assessed by asking the child to name the letters presented (in non-alphabetic order) on a card in both upper and lower case. A response should be scored as correct if the child gives the alphabetic name, the phonic label, or names a word that begins with the appropriate letter, for example z = zebra.

Assessing Knowledge of Rhyme and Phonology

This is a much more complex matter as slight changes in the task can greatly increase the ease or difficulty for the child.

Pre-school children can be assessed by observation for what is known as implicit knowledge of rhyme and alliteration. This is the ability to recite nursery rhymes and spontaneously to produce rhyme and alliteration. Conscious explicit knowledge of rhyme and alliteration can be assessed by asking children to pick the odd one out from a group of words, for example:

bus, bat, cow, boy (alliteration)
big, pig, jig, cow (rhyme)

Many workers have found that four words tax the auditory memory of young children and only use three words. It has also been found that the task can be made easier by using picture cards so that the child does not have to remember the words while thinking about the discrimination. Minor differences such as whether the initial consonant in the alliteration task precedes a vowel or is part of a consonant cluster affect the difficulty of the task, for example:

brush, blue, crow, blush (more difficult)
bus, bat, cow, boy (less difficult)

Testing Concepts of Print

Marie Clay has described Concepts of Print tests which can be used with non-readers. The child is asked to point to certain features as the examiner reads a book. The test measures whether the child is familiar with concepts such as the correct orientation of the book, that the print, not the picture carries the message, left-right directional rules, awareness that written English consists of discrete words, and so on. This test is useful to assess the degree of knowledge that children have about books before entering school and to assess progress in the first year of teaching. Most children will have acquired all of these concepts by the age of six or so.

Assessment in the Early Years of Schooling

Tests of concepts of print, alphabetic knowledge and rhyme and phonology continue to be relevant and to have direct teaching implications until children have mastered these skills. Some children will continue to find difficulty with phonological tasks in Primary 2 and Primary 3. However, at the end of Primary 1 it should also be possible to assess children's actual reading skills.

Single Word Reading

The quickest and easiest way to test early reading skills is to administer a simple word recognition test. In the past, such tests were criticised as they consist of a list of single words preventing the use of syntactic or contextual cues and providing no measure of reading comprehension. However, it is now known that the correlation between reading accuracy and reading comprehension is so high in the early stages that measuring the ability to read single words out of context gives an excellent measure of overall reading skill. Good readers are characterised by the ability to read individual words.

Reading Nonsense Words

The ability to read nonsense words is a useful indicator of the child's developing ability to use alphabetic and phonological knowledge to decode words. It has been shown that this ability also correlates highly with reading attainment. The teacher can easily devise her own test at an appropriate level of difficulty. For example, the following three lists are of increasing difficulty.

1	2	3
dat	drit	strach
bek	strob	drough
fot	ched	chedish
sen	shill	crasting

Reading in Context

A range of tests assesses reading ability through graded passages of text and includes questions on reading comprehension. In general, results on these tests for any individual will mirror the results on single word reading tests. However, the teacher may also gain additional insights into the actual strategies used by the child in continuous reading. For example, it may become apparent that the child:

- is overdependent on picture cues
- ignores the print and attends largely to context
- makes no use of syntactic cues
- does not self-correct decoding mistakes in the light of sentence meaning
- is overdependent on sounding out individual phonemes
- has difficulty with short function words

Occasionally, children will produce reasonable reading accuracy scores but poor comprehension scores. This is likely to be due to either an inadequate reading speed (the child decodes the print accurately but with such difficulty that he loses the sense of the passage) or because of inadequate language skills. If a child has difficulty with reading comprehension, it is worth reading a passage to the child and asking the comprehension questions. If they continue to have difficulty, it is likely that their spoken language skills require further investigation. If their performance improves greatly, it is likely that their difficulties are at the word identification level.

Reading can also be assessed through the use of class readers. Many of the above skills and attainments can be assessed in the course of normal reading instruction. It is also initially important to assess the level of difficulty of the text that the child is being asked to read. A child should be able to read 85–95 per cent of words correctly after normal tuition. If the child cannot do this, the book is not at an appropriate level.

Spelling

Spelling is easily assessed through a range of commercially available tests. Normally reading and spelling skills will develop in parallel. Children whose reading scores are reasonable in the early years, but who have very poor spelling may be over-reliant on visual memory and may require more help with learning the rules and common structures of printed words. Such children are likely to have difficulty reading nonsense words.

Planning Issues in Early Intervention

Before beginning work on an early intervention initiative it is recommended that staff discuss the following issues:

Staff Development

To ensure a whole school approach it is advisable that all members of staff attend development sessions and are provided with details of the recommendations for classroom practice.

Curriculum

When embarking on an early intervention programme it must be accepted that the amount of time spent on literacy activities will increase. There must be a commitment to a balanced approach to the teaching of reading which will include an appropriate emphasis at the early stages on concepts of print, phonological awareness, knowledge of letters and letter patterns and phonics. Opportunities for independent writing are to be encouraged from the earliest stages and children should read on a daily basis.

Resources

It is important that recommended resources are made available for staff prior to the commencement of the project.

Parental Involvement

Strategies to promote parental involvement in children's acquisition of literacy skills are central to an early intervention initiative. Parents can be involved in a variety of ways, both at home and in school, and it is important that the aims of the project are shared with parents and that they are made aware of the approaches to the teaching of reading used within the school. Reading homework should be set on a regular basis.

Community Links and Involvement of Other Agencies

All available options to increase the amount of literacy activities and supervised reading with children should be considered. Where possible adults, including parents and members of the community, can be invited to assist with the project. Local agencies and groups already involved with the schools could make a commitment to helping promote literacy activities, for example running homework clubs, nursery rhyme clubs or paired reading meetings. Libraries, bookshops and local businesses may also be able to offer assistance.

Deployment of Staff

Schools which have allocated learning support staff to Primary 1 and 2 stages have found this prioritisation to be very effective. It is therefore recommended that, where necessary, a review of the deployment of learning support staff within the school is undertaken. It may be that there are other staff within the school who could, for the duration of the project, focus their work at the early stages.

Reading Recovery

It has been repeatedly shown that a short 12–14 week intensive intervention based on Marie Clay's Reading Recovery programme offered to Primary 2 pupils leads to rapid improvements in attainment. This can be delivered with minimal training by experienced learning support teachers. It is, of course, difficult for schools to allocate the necessary time (30 minutes per day per pupil plus preparation time) from within the current learning support allocations. However, intervention at this stage is far more effective than traditional programmes of remediation. Assessment is integrated into the Reading Recovery programme.

Assessment

It is essential that there is 'before and after' testing of the pupils' attainment in literacy, with appropriate control group data gathered prior to the intervention. If schools wish to embark on more detailed assessments, advice is available in this handbook.

In-school Coordinator

It is recommended that a member of staff is designated to oversee the implementation of the project and to liaise with any outside agencies involved with the project.

Regular Review Meetings

It is recommended that regular meetings are planned for staff to share ideas and resources, discuss issues arising and to reflect upon their practice and any changes they have made during the implementation of the project.

Books and Materials

Essential Resources
Alphabet Frieze

Alphabet Mat

Alphabet Books

Rhyming Books

Rhyming Books and Tapes

Word, Letter and Picture Cards

Big Books

Letters (plastic, magnetic, wooden, foam, etc)

Clay, Marie M 1996 *Reading Recovery: A guidebook for teachers in training*, Auckland, NZ, Heinemann

Lloyd, Sue 1992 *The Phonic Handbook*, Essex, Jolly Learning

Rime and Analogy materials from *Oxford Reading Tree* which include Big Rhyming Books, Word and Picture Cards, Tapes, Rime and Analogy Games, Photocopy Masters and Teachers' Handbook (Oxford University Press).

Further Reading
Adams, Marilyn Jager 1990 *Beginning to Read: The new phonics in context,* Oxford, Heinemann

Adams, Marilyn Jager 1990 *Beginning to Read: Thinking and learning about print,* Cambridge, MA, MIT Press

Beard, Roger 1993 *Teaching Literacy: Balancing Perspectives,* London, Hodder & Stoughton

Bryant, Peter & Bradley, Lynette 1985 *Children's Reading Problems*, Oxford, Blackwell

Campbell, Robin 1995 *Literacy in Nursery Education*, Stoke-on-Trent, Trentham Books Ltd

Clay, Marie M 1985 *The Early Detection of Reading Difficulties*, Auckland, NZ, 3rd edition, Heinemann

Goswami, U & Bryant, P 1990 *Phonological Skills and Learning to Read*, Hillsdale, NJ, Lawrence Erlbaum Associates

Hall, Nigel & Robinson, Anne 1995 *Exploring Writing and Play in the Early Years*, David Fulton Publishers, London

Lothian Regional Council 1995 *A Policy for Reading*, Edinburgh

Lothian Regional Council 1995 *A Policy for Reading – Staff Development Materials*, Packs 1, 2 and 3, Edinburgh

Lothian Regional Council 1996 *That's My Letter*, Edinburgh

Owen, Pamela & Pumphrey, Peter 1995 *Children Learning to Read*, Vol 1, London, The Falmer Press

SOEID 1996 'Methods of Teaching Reading', *Interchange* No 39

COSTUME

Hats, Gloves & Footwear

Helen Whitty
POWERHOUSE MUSEUM

Heinemann
LIBRARY

www.heinemann.co.uk/library
Visit our website to find out more information about **Heinemann Library** books.

To order:
☎ Phone 44 (0) 1865 888066
🖹 Send a fax to 44 (0) 1865 314091
💻 Visit the Heinemann Bookshop at www.heinemann.co.uk/library to browse our catalogue and order online.

First published in Great Britain in 2001 by Heinemann Library, Halley Court, Jordan Hill, Oxford OX2 8EJ, a division of Reed Educational and Professional Publishing Ltd. Heinemann is a registered trademark of Reed Educational & Professional Publishing Limited.

OXFORD MELBOURNE AUCKLAND JOHANNESBURG BLANTYRE
GABORONE IBADAN PORTSMOUTH NH (USA) CHICAGO

First published 2000 by
MACMILLAN EDUCATION AUSTRALIA PTY LTD
627 Chapel Street, South Yarra, Australia 3141

Cover designed by Joanna Sapwell
Interior designed by Polar Design Pty Ltd
Illustrated by Wendy Arthur
Printed in China

ISBN 0 431 14423 0 (hardback)   ISBN 0 431 14430 3 (paperback)
05 04 03 02 01   05 04 03 02 01
10 9 8 7 6 5 4 3 2 1   10 9 8 7 6 5 4 3 2 1

British Library Cataloguing in Publication Data

Whitty, Helen
    Hats, gloves and footwear. – (Costume)
    1. Footwear 2. Gloves 3. Hats
    I. Title
    391.4'1

Cover photographs reproduced with permission of Powerhouse Museum, Sydney, Australia; and Ros and John Moriarty, Balarinji Design Studio, Australia (painted sandshoes).

Any words appearing in the text in bold, **like this**, are explained in the Glossary.

Contents

Introduction   4

Hats   6

   Types of hats   6
   Meet Rosie Boylan, milliner   12
   Make a hat   14

Gloves   16

   Gloves and mittens   16
   Muffs   18
   Hand puppets   20
   The Nintendo® Power Glove   21

Footwear   22

   Types of shoes   22
   Shoe timeline, 1700–1880   26
   Parts of a shoe   27
   How a shoe is made by hand   28
   Stockings and socks   29

Clothes for heads, hands and feet   30
   Answers   30
Glossary   31
Index   32
   Photo credits   32

> **Don't turn this page!**
> Think of all the things you wear on your head, hands and feet. See if you recognize any of them in this book.

Introduction

The things you wear on your body are your costume. You probably have things you like to wear and things you have to wear. Your family probably likes you to wear special clothes for certain occasions. Sometimes what you like to wear and what your family wants you to wear are very different. Have you heard someone say, 'I wouldn't be caught dead in that dress/jacket/hat/shoes'? People can feel very strongly about what they, and others, wear.

▼ 'FUNK INC' poster from funkessentials, designed in 1993

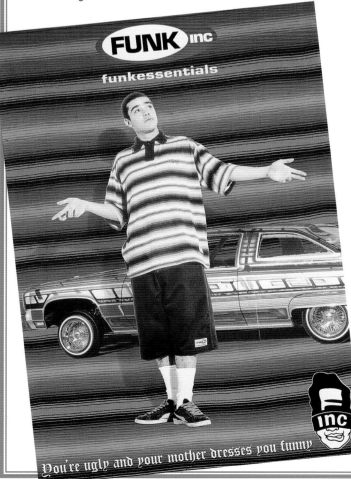

The story of costume is about people's creativity and the ways they like to show it. What people make, wear and care about are examples of this creativity. What people wear says something about them. *Costume* looks at wearing and making clothes across times, places and cultures.

Don't get dressed up to read this book – just dust off your imagination. Start off by imagining yourself without costume.

Too revealing? The strange thing is, the more you cover up with costume, the more you are really saying about yourself.

► Transparent plastic figure of a woman. It is full size, and shows the body organs, veins and arteries. It was made in 1954 to teach people about health and hygiene.

Hats, gloves and footwear

Hats, gloves and shoes are all the things you can wear on your head, hands and feet. Is this correct? What about **agals**, **aigrettes**, beanies, **balaclavas** and **tiaras** OR mittens, **muffs** and power gloves OR boots, loafers, moccasins, pumps, trainers and slippers? There are many different things you can wear on these parts of your body. You will see some of them in this book.

▶ 'Mary don't ask' wearable sculpture by Peter Tully, Australia, 1984. This outfit has things hung, draped, wrapped and layered all over the body, including the head, hands and feet. Is that headpiece a hat, telephone or tea cup?

Types of hats

There are many different types of hats. Some of them have special names.

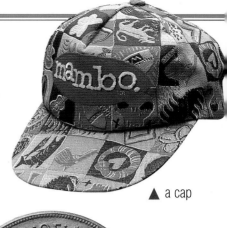

▲ a cap

▲ a crown

◀ an agal

▲
◀ hats
▼

a tiara ▶

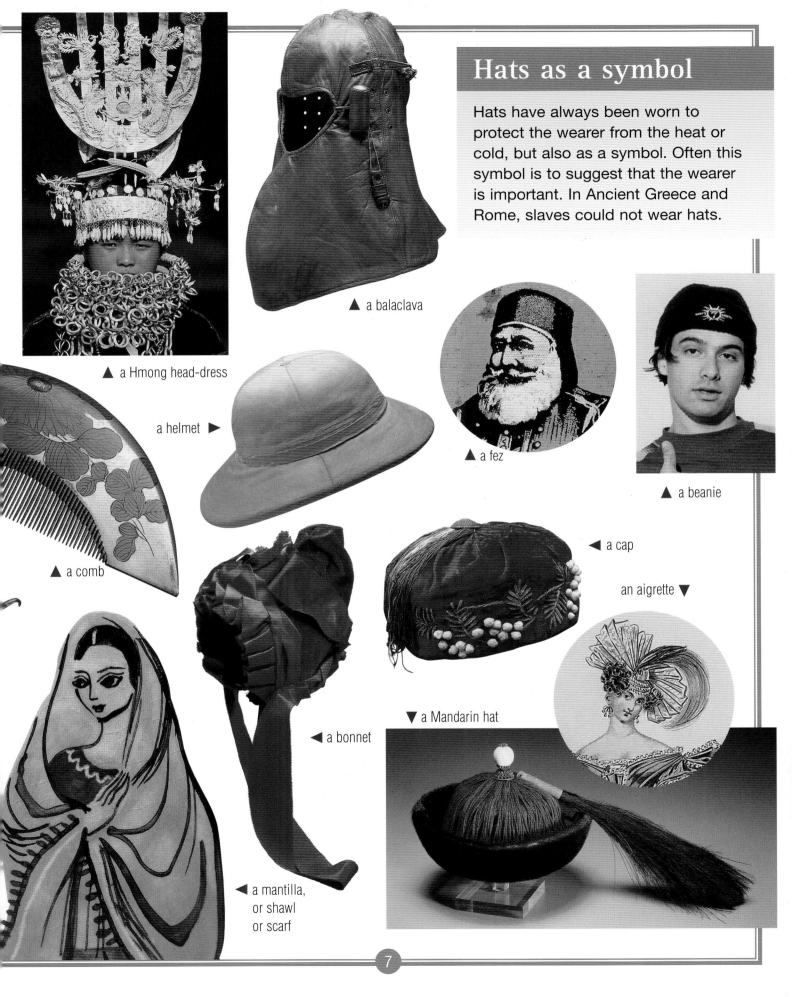

▲ a Hmong head-dress

▲ a balaclava

Hats as a symbol

Hats have always been worn to protect the wearer from the heat or cold, but also as a symbol. Often this symbol is to suggest that the wearer is important. In Ancient Greece and Rome, slaves could not wear hats.

a helmet ▶

▲ a fez

▲ a beanie

▲ a comb

◀ a cap

an aigrette ▼

◀ a bonnet

▼ a Mandarin hat

◀ a mantilla,
or shawl
or scarf

Hats made from plants

Hats can be made from materials that are found easily and cheaply, such as plants.

Bamboo

This hat is made of bamboo and gold paper, and is lined with newspaper. It comes from a village on the north coast of Java, Indonesia.

Gourd

This hat is made from a **gourd**, which is like a pumpkin. Inside, it has a woven bamboo shape to fit the head. It was made in the Philippines.

Cabbage-tree hat

Early colonists in Australia wanted hats made of straw like they had in Europe, but straw was not available. Instead, they used **fronds** from the cabbage-tree palm. These were cut into strands and woven to make hats to protect them from the sun.

Coconut

This hat was also made in the Philippines. It is made from coconuts.

▲ A cabbage-tree hat

'Virtual' hats

The **headset** in this picture makes the wearer feel as if they are in another world – a virtual reality. 'Virtual reality' means 'as if it were real'. You may experience something like this when you play a game with your friends and make up an imaginary world, or when you play games on your computer and see another world on screen. The headset below feeds very accurate sounds and pictures from a computer to the wearer's ears and eyes. The screen image is inescapable (unless you take off the headset). This is called an **'immersive** experience'. Whichever way the headset wearer looks, they see a 'view' of the virtual world.

▼ This immersive headset creates a 'virtual reality' for the wearer.

Caps

A cap for a married woman

This cap was made during the 1800s in Eastern Europe. This was a time when you could tell if a woman was married by what she wore on her head. After the wedding ceremony, another ceremony was performed where the wedding head-dress was exchanged for an embroidered cap. It was usually made from hand-spun **linen**, with a hand-embroidered pattern and crochet edging. Married women sang songs and carried candles while circling the new bride. The cap was to protect the woman from bad luck and she was always to wear it.

Unfortunately, the cap and hairstyle which went with it could rub the back of the head bald! These sorts of caps are now only worn at festivals as part of the traditional costume.

What they were wearing then

Sir Douglas Mawson (1882–1958) was a brave and daring Antarctic explorer. He made his first trip to Antarctica in 1908 with Sir Ernest Shackleton. He was the first person to explore uncharted Antarctic coastlines. The Antarctic base of Mawson is named after him. The picture on the Australian $100 note is from a photograph of Mawson taken by Frank Hurley on the Mawson expedition of 1911. Mawson is wearing:

- a balaclava of hand-knitted wool
- a snow helmet made of **burberry** – a waterproof fabric.

Mawson on the Australian $100 note.

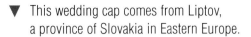
This wedding cap comes from Liptov, a province of Slovakia in Eastern Europe.

A decorated Kohistani child's cap

A decorated cap

This is another example of a cap made by hand. It was made sometime between 1930 and 1940 in Indus Kohistan in northern Pakistan. It was made from black cotton and silk, and red-printed floral cotton. The cap has an embroidered **geometric** design, with white beads, metal coins, and plastic and pearl buttons.

These caps were worn all the time in the cold mountain environment. The shape and decorations protected the wearer from the cold and from bad spirits.

Meet
Rosie Boylan,
milliner

▼ Rosie Boylan

How long have you been a milliner, Rosie?

I've been making hats about 16 years.

Didn't you do the hats for the Australian version of the musical *Cats*?

Everyone remembers that! I've also made hats for opera and films, such as *The Piano* and *Babe, Pig in the City*, and *The Phantom of the Opera*. Oh, and special events such as the galah head-dresses for the closing of the Olympic Games in Atlanta. I've made hats for individual clients. My hats have been all over the world and sat on all sorts of heads!

Tell us what is involved in making a hat for someone.

I meet with the client and find out what the hat will be used for. Is it for a special occasion like a wedding? Is it to wear in the garden to keep the sun off? I measure their head circumference above the brow and look at their height, head and body shape, proportion and colouring. I ask them what sort of decoration they might want – things like ribbons, flowers or bows. I think about the 'look' which will suit their personality.

What do you mean by colouring and proportion?

I look at the colour of their skin, eyes and hair and think about the colours of the hat which will complement their own colours. A hat with a great big brim would probably not suit the proportions of a short person – they might look like a mushroom…

Oh no!

I then look for materials and start doing the technical work – making the hat. At the next meeting with the client, we fit the hat and see how it suits them. Changing the height of the crown or width of the brim just a little can make a big difference. At the last

▼ The body (capeline) of a hat made from woven straw.

meeting, the client collects their hat with perhaps some small changes.

What do you use to make a hat?

I use steam to change the shape of materials, needles and thimbles, scissors, hat blocks and natural fibres.

What is the best part of your job?

In theatre or film, I like being drawn into the world being created. I like working as part of a team with interesting people to help make the characters fit into this world. I do this by making the hats which are just right for the character. With individual clients, the joy is having gone through a process with them to make a hat which brings their personality alive. They feel the hat is 'right' and so do I.

Make a hat

Pretend you are a milliner and make this hat for a friend.

What you need:

- felt, cardboard or stiff material
- scissors
- craft glue
- accessories such as flowers or cotton for stitching

Step 1

Interview your friend. Ask them what colours they would like, and how they would like their hat decorated.

Step 2

Measure the circumference of your friend's head. This will be the size of the crown.

Step 3

Cut out the brim, side and crown of the hat. Allow for a seam. The circumference of the crown should be at least three centimetres bigger than your friend's head and the same length as side D of the crown.

Step 4

Apply glue to the seamline of both the crown and inner edge of the brim at regular intervals.

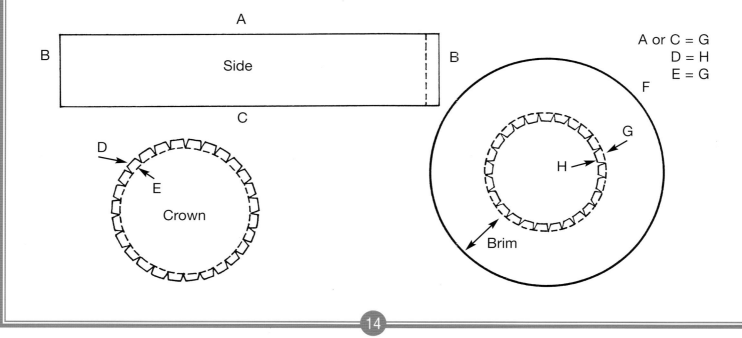

A or C = G
D = H
E = G

Step 5

Join the edges of the upright cylindrical section.

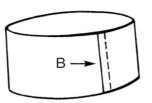

CHALLENGE 1

What do these sayings mean?
- I'll eat my hat.
- At the drop of a hat.
- To pass the hat around.
- A feather in your cap.

The answers are on page 30.

Step 6

Glue the tabs into position to join the crown to the upright section, making sure that the tabs are inside the hat.

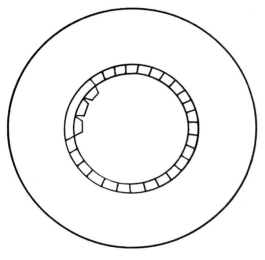

Step 8

Decorate the hat. In the examples shown, the black felt hat is oversewn with a blanket stitch and cross-stitch. There are crêpe-paper flowers on the pink cardboard hat. Or you could appliqué, embroider, or use artificial fruit, beads, braid, feathers or flowers.

Blanket stitch

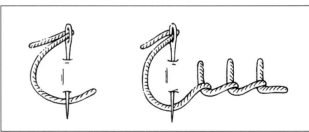

Cross-stitch

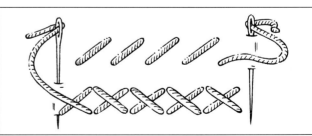

Step 7

Glue the tabs into position to join the brim to the upright section, making sure that the tabs are located inside.

15

Gloves and mittens

Archaeologists say that hand covers were worn by cave-dwellers hundreds of thousands of years ago. The cave dwellers' mittens were sewn with a needle made of bone. Knitted mittens have been found in Egyptian tombs. In ancient times, gloves were worn for both decoration and to protect the hands of workers. Later, warriors and hunters wore gloves. Gloves were also worn by kings and bishops to represent their power. Gloves are not only made to protect hands – they can be decorative.

▼ A pair of cream net lace mittens with satin drawstring ribbons

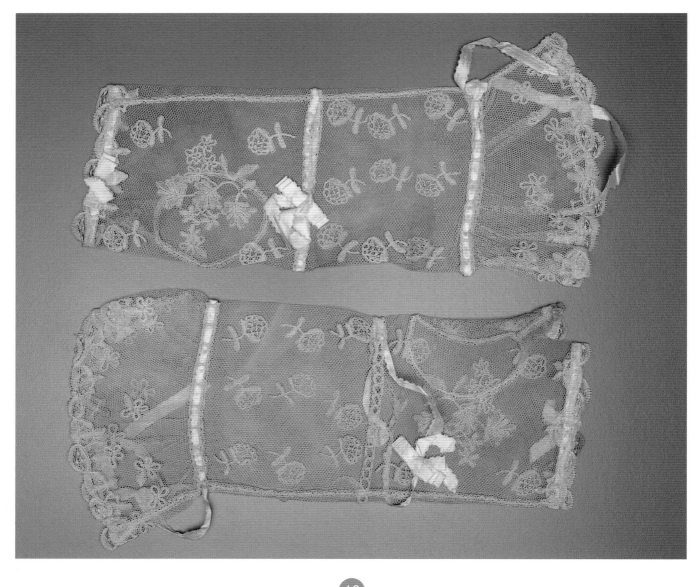

Messy Madeleine has six red woollen gloves and six green woollen gloves all mixed up in her drawer. What is the smallest number of gloves Madeleine has to pull out to be certain of getting a pair?

The answer is on page 30.

▲ Hand-knitted woollen gloves from around 1940

► Spanish or Italian **ecclesiastical** gloves made of knitted silk and silver metallic thread in the 1600s

Glove stories

- Gloves used to be exchanged when buying and selling land.
- Knights wore one of their lady's gloves on their breast as a sign of love.
- Hundreds of years ago, when a young man married, he gave the father of his bride one of his gloves as a sign that he would take care of his daughter.
- Chinese people extend a gloved hand to mean they are pleased to see you. In other cultures, you must remove your glove before offering your hand.

Muffs

Muffs are soft bags that open at both ends. They were used by men, women, boys and girls to warm their hands and to carry things such as hair combs and even small dogs! They were first used in France around 400 years ago. From around 200 years ago, muffs were mostly worn by women and girls, until the early 1900s when they became less fashionable.

This muff is made of **swansdown**. It is pure white and must have been very difficult to keep clean.

This child's muff was made around 1880. It is red velvet with a red silk corded strap. It has a red velvet bonnet to match.

This muff was made of animal fur, silk and linen between 1850 and 1900.

Matching sets

At the height of their popularity in the 19th century, muffs were an important accessory. They could be designed as a set with other accessories, or even to match the trim of a dress.

▲ This doll with its muff is from the 1920s.

► A Victorian child's bonnet and muff made of red velvet

Hand puppets

Glove puppets are one of the most common types of puppet. They are also one of the easiest puppets to make – they are basically a glove shape, decorated to create characters. They fit on the hand and are worked by the fingers to make the characters look as if they are moving or talking.

These two glove puppets, one a koala bear and the other a penguin, were mace in 1945.

The Nintendo® Power Glove

▶ The Nintendo® Power Glove

The Nintendo® Power Glove electronically tracks the wearer's movement. It was first used in 1989 to play Nintendo® video games. Instead of a joystick, the power glove controlled the action on the screen. It has strips of plastic printed with special ink along the back of the glove. There is a small **transmitter** close to the fingers.

21

Types of shoes

> 'The silver shoes,' said the Good Witch, 'have wonderful powers. And one of the most curious things about them is that they can carry you to any place in the world in three stages, and each stage will be made in the wink of an eye. All you have to do is to knock the heels together three times and command the shoes to carry you wherever you wish to go.'
>
> From *The Wonderful Wizard of Oz*
> by L. Frank Baum, 1900

Feet, like hands, are an important part of the body. Our feet need protection. But as with hats and gloves, we wear shoes for other reasons as well. Shoes have a practical purpose but are also an object of beauty.

◄ A man's shoe made of black suede with a thick tread synthetic sole, designed by Mambo Graphics, Australia, 1992

◄ A man's boot made of leather, metal, rubber and synthetic material, designed by Dirk Bikkembergs, Belgium, 1996

► A pair of women's shoes made of plastic, synthetic material and metal, designed by Mary Quant, around 1960–64

▲ A pair of shoes made of canvas, rubber and cotton, with a handpainted design on them by Balarinji Design Studio, Australia, 1995

▲ A pair of women's shoes called 'Portrait of a Slipper IV' by Donna-May Bolinger, Australia, 1993

Tiger shoes

The shoes pictured below are children's slip-on shoes appliquéd with fabric pieces and embroidered to look like tigers. Made by hand in China some time between 1900 and 1950, these shoes give enjoyment to their owner and also good luck! The tiger is a Chinese symbol of courage and bravery.

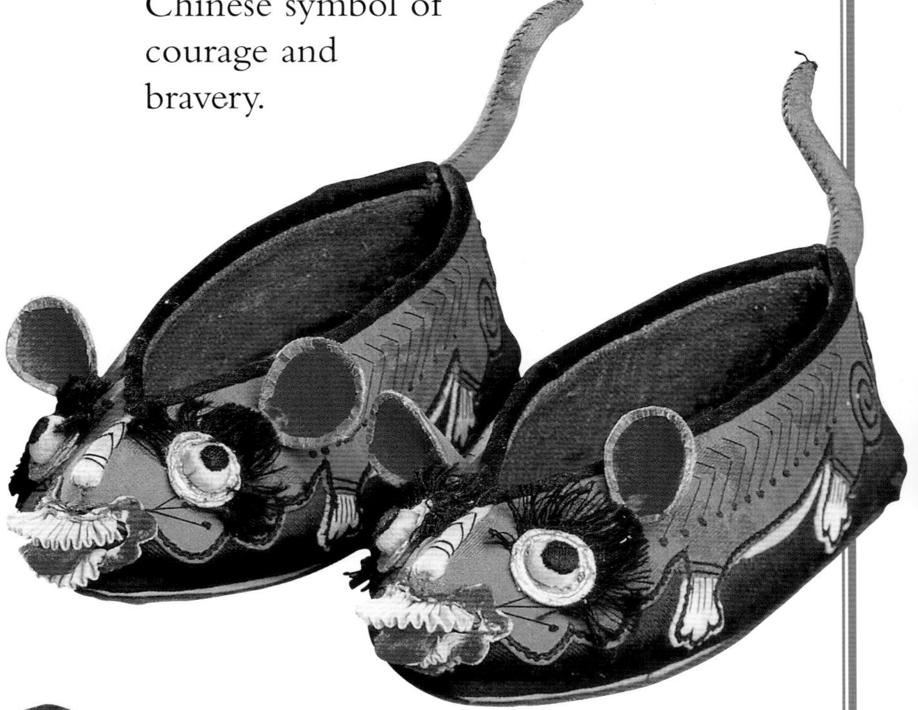

▲ Chinese tiger shoes

Lucky shoes

The hidden shoe

The shoe pictured below was found in 1904 hidden in the wall of a house in England. The style of the shoe suggests it was made in the early 1700s. During the 1700s, shoes were used as charms to ward off bad luck.

▶ The hidden shoe

▼ Ferragamo shoes

Golden shoes

These sandals were made by a famous Italian shoemaker called Salvatore Ferragamo in 1938. He padded the straps and covered the cork platform with hand-painted silk and tiny glass beads. They look very luxurious. However, he made them only out of materials available to him. He said there was 'no end to the materials a shoemaker may use to decorate his creations'.

Musical shoes

There are many songs about shoes. Do you know any of these?
- 'Boots of Spanish Leather' (Bob Dylan)
- 'These Boots are Made for Walking' (Nancy Sinatra)
- 'Blue Suede Shoes' (Elvis Presley)
- 'Put on Your Dancing Shoes' (Cliff Richard)
- 'Old Brown Shoe' (The Beatles)
- 'Sailing Shoes' (Little Feat)
- 'Put my Little Shoes Away' (Everly Bros)
- 'Walk a Mile in my Shoes' (Joe South)
- 'Golf Shoes' (Mental as Anything)
- 'Soul Shoes' (Graham Parker)
- 'Hi Heel Sneakers' (Jose Feliciano)
- 'Who's Gonna Fill Their Shoes?' (George Jones)
- 'Doctor Martin Boots' (Alexei Sayle)
- 'No Shoes' (John Lee Hooker)
- 'My Walkin' Shoes' (The Nitty Gritty Dirt Band)
- 'Goody Two Shoes' (Adam Ant)
- 'Knockin' Boots' (Candyman)
- 'Oh, Dem Golden Slippers' (African American spiritual)
- 'The Cobbler's Song' (Norton–Asche)

Shoe timeline, 1700–1880

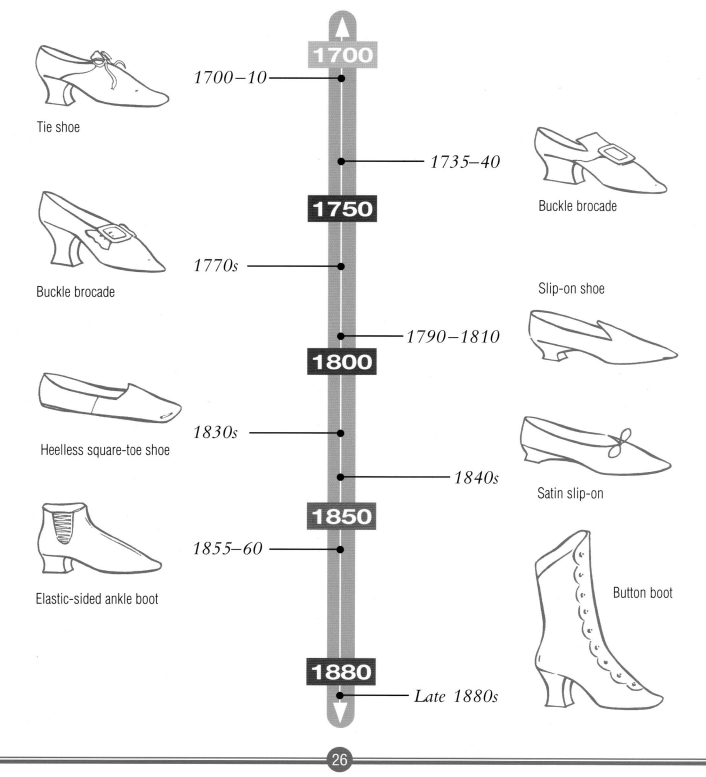

Tie shoe

Buckle brocade

Heelless square-toe shoe

Elastic-sided ankle boot

1700

1700–10

1735–40

Buckle brocade

1750

1770s

Slip-on shoe

1790–1810

1800

1830s

1840s

Satin slip-on

1850

1855–60

1880

Late 1880s

Button boot

Parts of a shoe

Lining

Tongue

Vamp

Toe cap

Innersole

Quarter

Heel

Welt

Sole

Many kinds of footwear

Footwear: *see* artics; balmoral; batts; bal; Blucher; boots; bottine; bulgha; carbattine; culiga; chopines; chukka; cockers; escapin; espadrille; gaiter; galoshes; geta; huaraches; jackboot; juliet; kamiks; krepis; larrigan; loafer; moccasins; mule; oxford; pattens; pedule; pegged boot; poulaines; pump; rubbers; sandals; scuffers; scuffs; shoes; slings; slippers; sneakers; solleret; tips; tsaruchia.

From *The Dictionary of Costume* by R. Turner Wilcox, BT Batsford Ltd, Great Britain, 1992

CHALLENGE 3

Find each of these shoes on the timeline.

1

2

3

4

5

6

The answers are on page 30.

How a shoe is made by hand

Step 1

The basis for all shoe making is a wooden model of a foot, known as a **last**. It is used to make a paper pattern of the shoe. Two lasts are made – one for each foot.

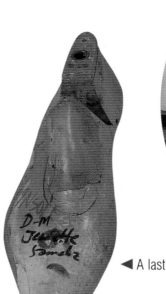

◄ A last

▲ Shoe designer Donna-May Bolinger in her studio

Step 2

Leather is then cut from the pattern for the upper, lining, sole and innersole of the shoe.

Step 3

The pieces of the upper are joined, along with the calf-skin lining.

Step 4

A 'stiffener' is slipped between the leather and the lining at the quarter. A firm 'toe puff' is used to fix the shape of the toe.

Step 5

All the edges are trimmed.

Step 6

The innersole and upper are fitted to the last, and tacked together.

Step 7

Strong linen thread is used to replace the tacks and joins the upper to the innersole.

Step 8

The sole is attached to the shoe.

Step 9

The heel is attached. It is often made of leather.

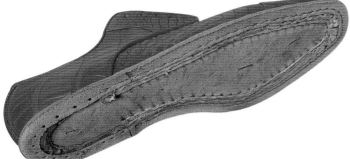

Stockings and socks

One of the socks below does not fall down when you walk. It has more elastic woven in the ankle than at the top so that it 'pushes up' as you walk.

This stocking was made by a 12-year-old girl for an exhibition of women's industries in 1888. It was made of cotton with fancy knitting at the top and foot.

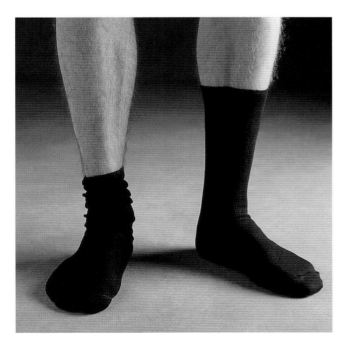

◄ A child's stocking from Holland, 1888

▲ The navy blue sock on the right is a 'Holeproof Computer sock', made of wool and nylon by Holeproof Socks Pty Ltd, Melbourne, 1990.

Clothes for heads, hands and feet

This book is full of interesting and delightful examples of costume that covers heads, hands or feet. These types of costume are called 'accessories' – things that assist the way we look. However, as you can see, some of the accessories in this book not only assist, they are essential!

Coverings for heads, hands and feet can warm the body, shield it from the sun, and protect it from sharp sticks and stones and harmful chemicals. Throughout history and in some cultures, these coverings had to be worn not only for protection but because the wearers were obeying social rules.

Coverings for heads, hands and feet protect us and say something about us. These coverings decorate our bodies. They show how creative we can be.

These shoes from the late 1930s are covered in hand-knitted material.

CHALLENGE 4

In this book are other pairs of shoes decorated with flower patterns. See if you can find them.

The answer is below.

Answers

Page 15

'I'll eat my hat' means that you do not believe what someone is telling you.

'At the drop of a hat' means that you will do something quickly or perhaps unexpectedly.

'To pass the hat around' means that you are collecting money, probably for a gift.

'A feather in your cap' means that you have received a reward.

Page 17

Madeleine has to pull three gloves out to make sure she gets a pair.

Page 27

Shoe 1 is a tie shoe from 1700–10.

Shoe 2 is a button boot from the late 1880s.

Shoe 3 is a heelless square-toe from the 1830s.

Shoe 4 is a slip-on from 1790–1810.

Shoe 5 is buckle brocade shoe from the 1770s.

Shoe 6 is a satin slip-on shoe from the 1840s.

Page 30

Shoes on page 24 and shoe 5 on page 27 are decorated with flower patterns.

Glossary

agal   hoops of thick cord, wool or goat's hair that hold the 'Kaffiyeh', or cloth of an African head-dress, in place

aigrettes   plumes, or tufts of plumes, made from feathers and used as a European woman's head-dress

balaclava   knitted cap that pulls down over the head and under the chin

burberry   a cloth treated to make it waterproof and used to make overcoats and suits

ecclesiastical   a descriptive word meaning something to do with the church

fronds   the divided leaves of plants such as ferns and palms

geometric   a descriptive word for something that has mathematical shapes such as squares and triangles

gourd   the fruit of a climbing plant. The shell of this fruit can be dried and used as a container or a head covering

headset   a device that fits over the head. It is generally used for listening to a radio but can be connected to a computer for images and sound.

immersive   to be surrounded by another world

last   a mould or wooden form over which a shoe is built

linen   fabric made from a flax plant

milliner   person who makes or sells hats

muffs   soft bags that open at both ends, used to keep the hands warm

papier-mâché   a strong substance made of paper pulp mixed with glue

swansdown   fine soft feathers from a swan

tiara   piece of jewellery that looks like a crown and is worn on the head

transmitter   a machine for broadcasting or sending a message

Index

A

agals 5, 6
aigrettes 5, 7

B

balaclavas 5, 7, 10
beanies 5, 7
bonnets 7, 19

C

caps 6, 10–11
combs 7
countries
  Australia 8
  China 17, 23
  Egypt 16
  France 18
  Indonesia 8
  Italy 24
  Pakistan 11
  Philippines 8
  Slovakia 11
crochet 10
crowns 6

D

decoration 13
designers and artists
  Bolinger, Donna-May 28–9
  Boylan, Rosie 12–13
  Ferragamo, Salvatore 24
  Mambo 6, 22

E

Eastern Europe 10
embroidery 10, 11, 23

F

fezzes 7

G

glove puppets 20
gloves 16–17

H

hats 6–15
head-dresses 7
headsets 9
helmets 7

M

mantillas 7
materials
  cotton 29
  fur 18
  lace 16
  leather 28, 29
  linen 10, 18, 29
  plants 8
  silk 17, 18, 24
  velvet 18, 19
milliners 12–13
mittens 5, 16, 17
muffs 5, 18–19

P

power gloves 5, 21

S

shoes 22–9
socks 29
stockings 29

T

tiaras 6

Photo and object credits

All objects featured in this publication are from the Powerhouse Museum collection and all photographs are by the Powerhouse Museum, unless otherwise indicated below. Collection objects are reproduced by permission of the designers or makers listed. The museum acknowledges the many generous donations of objects, which form a significant part of its collection.

p3 'Portrait' shoes by Donna-May Bolinger; p4 funkessentials poster by Sara Thorn and Bruce Slorach 1993; p5 'Mary don't ask' by Peter Tully 1984, permission Merlene Gibson; pp6/7 (clockwise from top left) feathered hat by Philip Treacy, Mambo cap by Gerry Wedd for Mambo Graphics Pty Ltd, Hmong head-dress photo by Fong Siu Nang, funkessentials beanie by Sara Thorn and Bruce Slorach, shawl drawing on ceramic by Martin Boyd Pottery, 'Marinara tiara' by Dinosaur Designs; p9 immersive head set photo, Cybermind UK Ltd; p10 $100 bill, Reserve Bank of Australia; p17 woollen gloves by Myra Mogg; p22 'Wunala Dreaming' shoes by Ros and John Moriarty, Balarinji Design Studio 1995, Mambo shoes by Mambo Graphics Pty Ltd; p23 'Portrait' shoes by Donna-May Bolinger, Australia, 1993; p24 shoes by Ferragamo; p29 Computer socks photo, Holeproof; p30 shoes by Myra Mogg 1930s.

Please visit the Powerhouse Museum at **www.phm.gov.au**